Everything You Need to Know About

When Someone You Know Has Leukemia

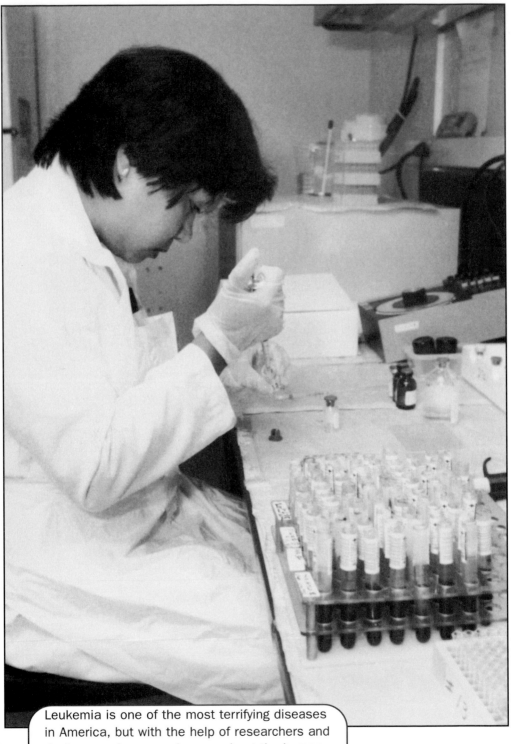

Leukemia is one of the most terrifying diseases in America, but with the help of researchers and doctors, we know much more about the human body and how cancer forms than ever before.

Everything You Need to Know About When Someone You Know Has Leukemia

Heather Moehn

The Rosen Publishing Group, Inc.
New York

Published in 2000 by The Rosen Publishing Group, Inc.
29 East 21st Street, New York, NY 10010

Copyright © 2000 by The Rosen Publishing Group, Inc.

First Edition

Library of Congress Cataloging-in-Publication Data

Moehn, Heather.
    Everything you need to know when someone you know has leukemia / Heather Moehn.
    p. cm. — (The need to know library)
    Includes bibliographical references and index.
    Summary: Discusses the causes, diagnosis, and treatment of leukemia and explains to provide physical and emotional support for its victims.
    ISBN 0-8239-3121-8 (lib. bdg.)
    1. Leukemia—Juvenile literature. 2. Leukemia—Psychological aspects—Juvenile literature. 3. Caregivers—Juvenile literature. [1. Leukemia. 2. Diseases.] I. Title. II. Series.

  RC643.M6245 1999
  616.99'419—dc21

                                                      99-047210

Manufactured in the United States of America

Contents

Introduction

*L*ori couldn't believe what her parents were telling her. They had just returned from the hospital where her little brother, Billy, had gone for some tests. He had been feeling sick for the past two weeks, but Lori didn't think anything of it. It just seemed like he had a bad case of the flu. Now her dad was saying that Billy had leukemia and that he would be in the hospital for a while. He would start chemotherapy soon and the doctors hoped that the cancer would go into remission. But he was going to be sick for a long time and there was no guarantee that he would get better.

Lori felt guilty for all the times that she had picked on her little brother. She also felt guilty because she was healthy while he was so sick. She *was angry that Billy had to deal with such an awful disease. And she was afraid that he was in a lot of pain and scared that he might die. She also had many questions. What exactly is leukemia? What causes it? Is it hereditary? Can I catch it?*

Lori's mom said that the family was going to meet with a counselor at the hospital tomorrow. The counselor would be able to answer their questions and help them learn how to deal with the disease. "It's going to be tough," she said, giving Lori a hug. "But we'll get through this together."

Cancer is one of the most terrifying words in the English language. It becomes even more frightening when someone you love has been diagnosed with a form of cancer. Decades ago, doctors didn't know very much about the disease and people avoided talking about it. Treatments were undeveloped and someone diagnosed with cancer usually died within a few years.

Today, doctors know much more about the human body and how cancer forms. Researchers constantly discover new methods and better drugs for fighting the disease. With treatments such as chemotherapy, radiation, and organ transplants, thousands of people each year are able to beat the disease and lead long, cancer-free lives.

If someone you know has recently been diagnosed

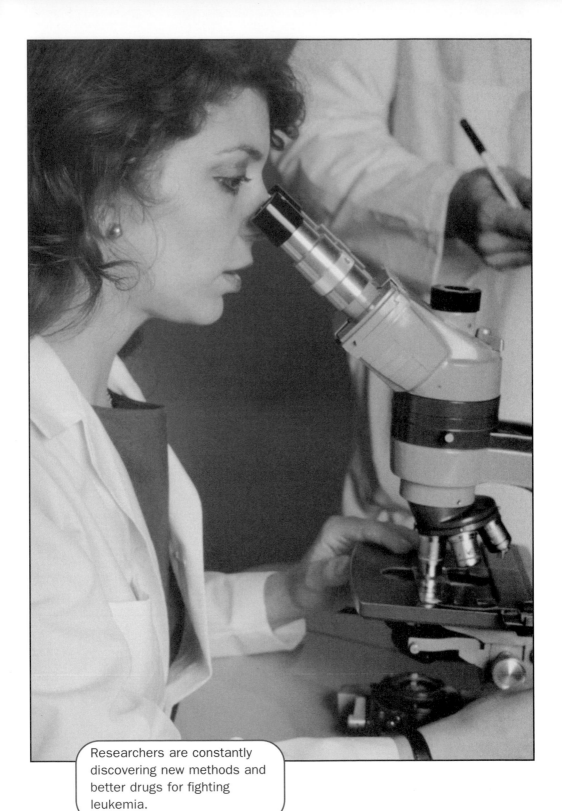

Researchers are constantly discovering new methods and better drugs for fighting leukemia.

with leukemia, you are probably experiencing emotions similar to Lori's. You probably also have many questions about the disease. This book will explain what leukemia is, how the disease is diagnosed, and what to expect during treatment. There is also a section on understanding your emotions and tips to help you get through the difficult times. Even though leukemia is a very serious disease, understanding it and knowing what to expect will make it seem much less frightening.

Chapter One

What Is Leukemia?

Before you can understand leukemia, it is important to know about cells and how they function. When a sperm and egg unite, a single cell is formed that contains twenty-three chromosomes from the father and twenty-three chromosomes from the mother. Thousands of genes are arranged along these forty-six chromosomes. These genes blend information from both parents and are the blueprint for the new person being formed. Genes are best known for deciding physical characteristics such as eye color, hair texture, and height. But this is only a small part of what they do. Genes also control cell functions like making sure that oxygen gets carried throughout the body, blood gets purified, and energy is extracted from food.

In the womb, that single cell quickly divides and

produces daughter cells that have the exact same genetic makeup. These cells and all their offspring quickly divide again and again until trillions of cells have formed. Every one of these cells has the exact same chromosomes and genes as the original.

How does this mass of identical cells then become a person? As the cells mature, some group together and become brain cells, others develop into liver cells, while others become blood cells. This process is called differentiation. In total, there are about 200 different kinds of cells in the human body. Each type has a specific job to do to keep the body functioning.

For the differentiated cells to perform properly, all of the genes can't be working at the same time. If they did, it would be complete chaos. Imagine if you had thousands of people telling you to do different things at the same time. You wouldn't be able to function. Instead, as cells differentiate, certain genes give instructions while all the rest remain silent. For example, in the liver, the genes that tell the cell to purify blood turn on, while the genes that make hair grow stay turned off.

In addition to knowing what genes should turn on in each cell, the genes also know when to start and stop working. Stem cells, whose job it is to create new cells when the old ones have died, are a good example. When they sense that more cells are needed, a mechanism turns on the genes that promote cell production.

When enough cells have been made, the genes are turned off again.

If you are baffled by the fact that trillions of little cells in your body know exactly what to do and when to do it, you are not alone. Scientists have spent decades trying to figure out how cells and genes work, and they still don't have complete answers. The closer they get to understanding the process, the better we will understand how and why cancer develops.

What Is Cancer?

Cancer forms when healthy cells are altered in such a way that the system of normal cell growth breaks down. Scientists believe that every person has a small number of genes, called oncogenes, in his or her cells that have the potential to turn normal cells into cancerous ones. When a person develops cancer, something occurs that causes the oncogenes to alter the genetic material of the cell.

As a result of this alteration, the cells do not know their job or how to perform properly. All they can do is reproduce and create other abnormal cells. These cells are very aggressive and compete with healthy cells for nutrients. Soon there are enough abnormal cells to interfere with the regular functions of organs. Without treatment, the cancer cells spread throughout the body, overpowering the healthy cells and eventually causing death.

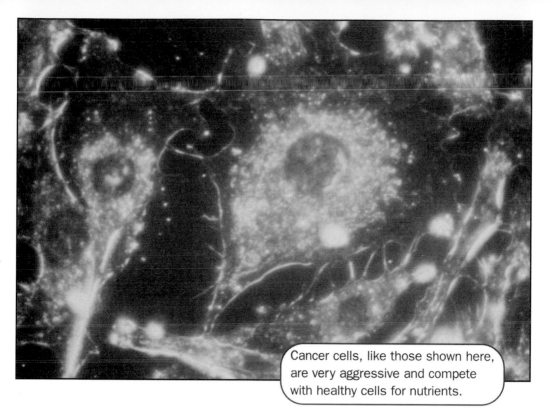

Cancer cells, like those shown here, are very aggressive and compete with healthy cells for nutrients.

The term "cancer" describes more than one hundred types of diseases that develop from abnormal cell growth. The kind of cancer that a person has depends upon the type of cell affected and the life stage it is in when it mutates, that is, becomes cancerous.

What Is Leukemia?

The term "leukemia" comes from a Greek word meaning "white blood. " It is a type of cancer that affects the blood-producing tissues.

In healthy people, blood cells develop and mature in the bone marrow. Bone marrow is a soft, fatty substance that fills the hollow space inside bones. Normally three types of cells are produced: red blood cells (RBCs), which carry oxygen around the body and help remove carbon dioxide; white blood cells (WBCs), which fight infections; and platelets, which form plugs to stop bleeding from injuries. The growth and development of these blood cells is carefully controlled so that the correct number of each type of cell is produced to keep the body healthy. RBCs have a life span of about four months, platelets live for a few days, and WBCs live only for a few hours. With this amount of turnover, approximately three million red blood cells and 120,000 white blood cells are produced every second.

In a person with leukemia, the control mechanism breaks down, and too many abnormal white blood cells are produced. These immature cells, known as lymphoblasts or blasts, cannot perform their normal function of fighting infections. Instead, they quickly reproduce, take over the bone marrow, invade the blood stream, and cause the person to become ill.

Who Gets Leukemia

Anyone can get leukemia. It strikes people of all ages and both sexes. Researchers estimate that there will be approximately 28,700 cases of leukemia diagnosed each year in the United States.

Because leukemia causes more deaths in children than any other disease, it is often thought of as a childhood illness. However, it actually affects ten times as

Anyone can get leukemia;
even young people.

many adults as children (2,200 cases in children 0–14 years old compared with 26,500 cases in adults, annually). Over half the total cases will be in people over the age of sixty-five.

The Different Types of Leukemia

There are several different kinds of leukemia. Each one has a characteristic way of behaving and requires a different treatment. Some types occur mostly in children while others only affect adults. Some develop rapidly while others progress slowly. The one thing all types of leukemia have in common is that they develop from the growth of abnormal white blood cells.

One way to classify the different kinds of leukemia is by the type of white blood cell involved. There are three kinds of WBCs that are created in the bone marrow and each one helps the body fight germs: granulocytes contain enzymes that break down foreign material; monocytes surround germs and digest them; lymphocytes fight infections. If the granulocytes or monocytes are involved, the leukemia is called myelogenous. If the leukemia develops in the lymphocytes, it is called lymphocytic.

A second method of classification is by the speed with which the disease progresses if it is left untreated. Acute leukemia develops quickly and the symptoms occur immediately. The WBCs are extremely immature and can be detected easily in the bloodstream. Because it progresses quickly and is usually diagnosed soon after it forms, acute leukemia is easier to treat and in many cases can be cured completely. Most childhood leukemias are acute.

Chronic leukemia, on the other hand, progresses much more slowly. The cells are more mature and closely resemble normal WBCs when they mutate. The symptoms may not show up for years after the disease begins to develop. Many people with some form of chronic leukemia are surprised to learn that they have the disease after a routine physical exam. Because it is often not detected until a late stage, chronic cases are harder to treat than the acute ones.

The names given to the different types of leukemia are descriptive of these classifications. In the four most common types, two are chronic and two are acute; two affect the lymphocytes, and two affect the granulocytes or monocytes. These four types will now be discussed in more detail.

Acute Lymphocytic Leukemia (ALL)

The most common type of leukemia found in children is acute lymphocytic leukemia (ALL). Because it progresses quickly, treatment usually begins immediately and is very aggressive. For some reason ALL affects more boys than girls and more white children than minorities. Forty percent of children with ALL are between the ages of three and five. This is the most treatable form of leukemia, with more than half of the patients cured.

ALL also accounts for a fifth of all leukemia cases in adults. The outlook for adults with ALL is not quite as good as for children—a cure is obtained in about a third of the cases. But even in cases where a complete cure is not possible, a remission is very likely and may be long lasting.

Acute Myelogenous Leukemia (AML)

Acute myelogenous leukemia (AML), also called acute nonlymphocytic leukemia (ANLL), is the second most common form of leukemia in children. It also affects a large percentage of adult patients. AML is common in babies during the first month of life. It is hardly ever seen in childhood, but becomes more frequent in teenagers and young adults. Once adults reach fifty-five years of age, AML is the most common form of acute leukemia. The treatments, like those for ALL, begin right away and are aggressive.

Chronic Lymphocytic Leukemia (CLL)

CLL is a slow-moving form of leukemia. A person can have CLL for years without any symptoms. Since it may take years to progress, it is typical for no treatment to be given until symptoms appear. Ninety percent of cases occur in people over the age of fifty. It accounts for a quarter or more of all leukemia cases.

This is a magnification of AML cells.

Chronic Myelogenous Leukemia (CML)

CML is the only form of chronic leukemia ever seen in children. However, it is very rare and accounts for only two percent of all childhood leukemia cases. It most often affects people who are over fifty years old. There are several phases of CML. The first is the chronic phrase in which the disease progresses slowly and the patient has few symptoms. This phase can last up to six years. During the next phase, called the accelerated phase, the number of blast cells in the bone marrow increases rapidly. These cells are very resistant to treatment. The final stage is when the blast cells spread into the blood stream. It is not known why CML becomes gradually more aggressive. Scientists think that perhaps additional gene alterations take place after the disease first forms.

Michael's grandmother, June, was shocked to learn after her annual exam that she had leukemia. She told her doctor she was feeling a little tired and run down, so he performed a routine blood test. He discovered that she had a high number of WBCs and a low number of RBCs and platelets. After further testing, he discovered that June had chronic lymphocytic leukemia. Because of the slow development of the disease, June had not experienced any symptoms. Since the disease was progressing so slowly, they decided to carefully monitor its development and wait before starting any treatment.

The Symptoms of Leukemia

Leukemia is hard to diagnose. People like June may have chronic leukemia for many years without any symptoms. In acute leukemia the symptoms are similar to many other illnesses. Doctors have to eliminate possibilities such as rheumatic fever and anemia before diagnosing leukemia.

John usually played football with his friends after school. But for the past few weeks he felt too tired to keep up with them. At first, his mother thought that his fever and paleness were caused by the flu. She became more concerned when she noticed that he had a scrape on his elbow that didn't heal, and several bruises on his arms and legs. When John didn't seem to get any better, she took him to the doctor. After several tests, the doctors determined that John had acute lymphocytic leukemia. Because it was an acute case, the symptoms developed immediately. John was immediately admitted to the hospital and treatment began the next day.

The early symptoms seem like those of a cold or the flu. A person with leukemia will probably be pale, weak and tired, and may run a slight fever. Anemia, a condition caused by a shortage of red blood cells, develops in almost all leukemia patients. Other signs include bruising easily, frequent nosebleeds, night sweats, and getting scrapes and cuts that do not heal. Sometimes small red dots, like a rash, appear on the skin.

As the disease progresses, the person will feel very tired and have high fevers. The liver, spleen, and lymph nodes swell and become very tender. Bones and joints usually ache and the gums might swell and start to bleed.

All these symptoms are caused by the increased number of abnormal white blood cells that fill the bone marrow and circulate in the blood stream. The immature WBCs do not leave enough room for the RBDs to supply the body with oxygen, so the patient feels tired and weak. Cuts do not heal and the nose bleeds because there are fewer platelets in the blood stream. The person often catches colds that last a long time because there are not enough fully mature WBCs to fight infections. Some people experience joint or bone pain because the abnormal cells move to the surface of the bones from the bone marrow.

These symptoms alone do not necessarily mean that a person has leukemia. They could be caused by a number of other disorders. The only way a doctor can accurately diagnose leukemia is with blood tests.

Chapter Two

The Causes of Leukemia

Leukemia results from damage to the genes that control blood cell growth, development, and division. No one knows for certain why these genes mutate or why this causes leukemia. As a result, it is impossible to tell who will develop the disease. Nor are there any preventative measures a person can take to help avoid the disease, like not smoking to prevent lung cancer or staying out of the sun to prevent skin cancer.

Doctors do know that leukemia is not caused by an earlier illness or by a fall or injury. It cannot be inherited by the children of leukemia patients. In fact, pregnant women with leukemia typically give birth to babies with no trace of the disease. It is also not contagious—you cannot catch leukemia from someone like you catch a cold or chicken pox. If a friend or family member has leukemia, you are not at risk.

Although the exact cause is not known, researchers have found that certain circumstances may lead to an increased chance that someone will develop the disease. Environmental factors, genetics, and viruses may play a role in the cell mutations that cause leukemia. However, it is important to remember that these circumstances are only potential risk factors. Many people who have been exposed do not develop the disease. And most people who have leukemia had none of the known risks. Until doctors better understand what causes the genes to mutate, the reason some people develop leukemia and others don't will remain a mystery.

Environmental Factors

Within the last few decades, people have become more aware of the effect the environment has on health. Research has proved that certain chemicals polluting the air, ground, and water will cause cancer. Today, much work has been done to clean up the earth. Strict laws about where companies can dump waste and what gases can be emitted into the air have helped to minimize some risks. Most of the chemicals known to cause leukemia, such as benzene, are not encountered in everyday life, and special safety precautions are taken when they are handled.

Exposure to ionizing radiation from radioactive material also increases the chances of getting leukemia.

Research has proved that certain chemicals polluting the air, ground, and water will cause cancer.

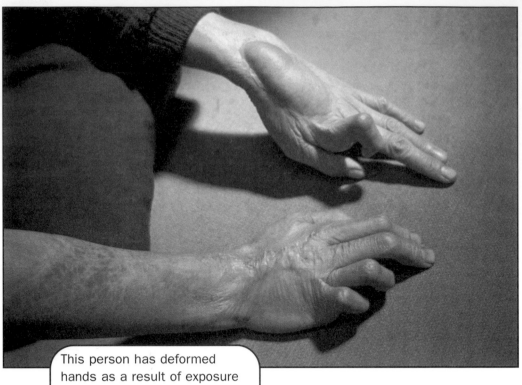

This person has deformed hands as a result of exposure to radiation.

One in six survivors of the Hiroshima atomic bomb explosion developed leukemia and people exposed to nuclear reactor accidents also have a higher incidence of the disease. In these cases, people were exposed to very high doses of radiation. Most experts agree that low levels of radiation probably don't cause leukemia.

Some studies suggest that electromagnetic fields (EMF), such as those associated with power lines or other electrical facilities, might cause leukemia. Statistics show a higher percentage of cases around EMF sites. However, there has been little evidence showing a direct link. As a precaution, the electrical industry has been reducing the strength of EMF around large transmission lines.

People who have been treated with radiation therapy and chemotherapy for other forms of cancer have an increased risk of developing leukemia five to eight years after the treatment. This is known as secondary leukemia. Leukemia that develops in this way is usually very difficult to treat because it is resistant to many drugs. Researchers are working on developing new types of drugs that minimize this risk. Most people agree that the benefits of cancer treatments outweigh the slight possibility of developing leukemia later in life.

Genetic Factors

Doctors have also found that certain disorders that affect chromosomes may increase the likelihood that the disease will develop. Children with Down's syndrome have three copies of chromosome 21 instead of two. For some reason they are fifteen times more likely to develop either ALL or AML than are other children. Males with an extra x chromosome (this is known as Kleinfelter's syndrome) also have an increased risk. Cases of CML in adults are often associated with an abnormal chromosome known as the Philadelphia chromosome.

Other disorders not related to chromosomes also lead to an increased risk. A medical condition called myelodysplasia, which usually affects older people, has been shown to make AML more common. This condition causes the bone marrow to stop producing normal amounts of RBCs, WBCs, and platelets. Other disorders linked with higher occurrences of leukemia include the Li-Fraumeni syndrome, neurofibromatosis, and ataxia telangectasia.

Viral Factors

Some types of leukemia that develop in animals, such as feline leukemia, Rous chicken sarcoma, and Rauscher mouse leukemia are known to be caused by a virus. This has lead many scientists to think that a virus may also cause human leukemia. They have found only one virus that might be responsible for some cases of leukemia. It is called the HTLV-1 and is found mainly in Japan and the Caribbean.

Chapter Three

Diagnosis and Treatment

I f doctors suspect that someone has leukemia, they must examine the blood of the patient under a microscope. They count the number of WBCs, RBCs, and platelets. People with leukemia have too many white blood cells and not enough RBCs or platelets. They also check for abnormal white blood cells called lymphoblasts.

Even if they find that the blood count suggests leukemia, the doctors cannot be certain until they perform a bone marrow test. This is done by removing a small amount of bone marrow from either the breastbone or the back of the hipbone. To remove the marrow, a long needle is inserted into the bone and the marrow is drawn out. This is called the aspiration method. The bone marrow is then examined for abnormalities.

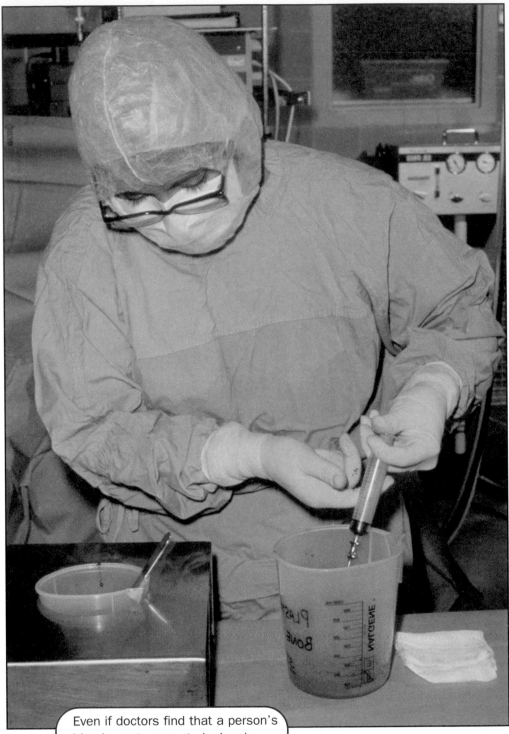

Even if doctors find that a person's blood count suggests leukemia, they cannot be certain until they perform a bone marrow test.

Erin was at the hospital for blood tests. Her friends and family were concerned because she had not been her usual peppy self for the past two weeks. Instead she felt very tired and had dark circles under her eyes. She complained that her bones ached and often woke in the middle of the night with a nosebleed.

Erin's doctor began with a routine physical examination. He took her temperature and found that Erin had a slight fever. He pressed on her abdomen and discovered that her liver and spleen were swollen. Erin showed him a cut on her knee that she had for over a month. From these symptoms, the doctor knew that leukemia was a possibility. However, there was not enough information yet to make an accurate diagnosis.

Next, the doctor took a little blood from Erin's finger to examine under a microscope. The results showed that there was a high number of WBCs and a low number of platelets and RBCs. Although this blood count could indicate leukemia, it also could result from a number of other illnesses, including a bad infection or anemia.

Further testing was needed, so the doctor performed a bone marrow aspiration. Erin was given a local anesthetic so she would not feel any pain. The doctor inserted a long needle into Erin's hipbone. He used the hipbone because it is *large and it is easy to remove bone marrow from that area. After the needle was in place, he used a syringe to suck the bone marrow out. When laboratory workers examined the bone marrow, they discovered a large number of leukemic blasts. The doctor now knew for certain that Erin had leukemia.*

Once it has been determined that the patient has leukemia, there are additional laboratory tests to determine the type. These additional tests may be necessary because in many cases the lymphoblasts are so abnormal and immature that it is impossible to tell what type of WBC they are.

Cytochemistry exposes the cells to stains or dyes. If the cells are from certain types of leukemia, the dyes cause them to turn different colors. For example, one stain causes parts of AML cells to appear black under a microscope. In flow cytometry, the cells are treated with special antibodies and passed in front of a laser beam. Each antibody sticks to a certain type of leukemia cell. If the sample contains those cells, the laser causes them to give off light. Immunocytochemistry also exposes cells to antibodies. But instead of giving off light, the antibodies cause certain kinds of leukemia cells to change colors.

After doctors have diagnosed that leukemia is present and determined the specific type, they perform more tests to determine how advanced the disease is

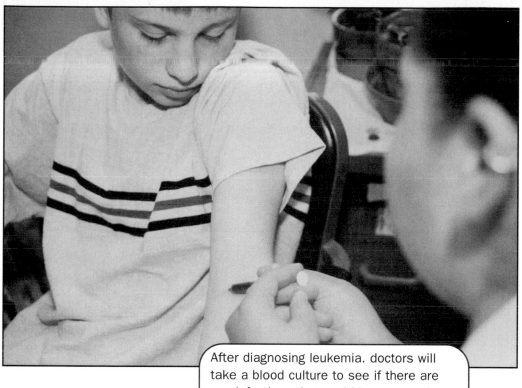

After diagnosing leukemia. doctors will take a blood culture to see if there are any infections that could become serious.

and to see if any complications have developed. They take blood, urine, and throat cultures to see if there are any infections that could become serious. They also perform kidney and liver tests to make sure that the cancer hasn't spread to these organs.

At this point, there will be a team of doctors working together to determine the proper diagnosis and decide upon a course of action. Besides the primary care physician, some types of doctors you might come in contact with include a pathologist, a doctor with special training in diagnosing diseases from laboratory tests; an oncologist, a doctor who specializes in treatment of cancer; and a hematologist, a doctor who specializes in blood diseases.

The Treatment of Leukemia

Treatment for acute leukemia begins as soon as possible after it is diagnosed. For chronic leukemia, it may begin immediately, or the doctors may wait to see how the disease progresses. The goal of treatment is to destroy all the cancer cells so there is no longer any trace of the disease anywhere in the body. Treatment also attempts to stop the cancer from spreading, to kill cancer cells if they have already spread to other parts of the body, and to slow its growth. There are three main types of treatment: chemotherapy, surgery, and radiation. Most people receive a combination of these three therapies.

Chemotherapy

The most common method of treating leukemia is chemotherapy. Because there are so many types of leukemia and because each person is affected differently, chemotherapy is very individualized. One person receiving chemotherapy is most likely getting different drugs and different doses than another person.

The treatment usually occurs in four stages. The first stage is called induction. For several months the patient is given large doses of very strong drugs to kill most of the cancer cells and put the cancer into remission. The second stage is known as consolidation or continuation therapy. It makes sure the cancer stays in

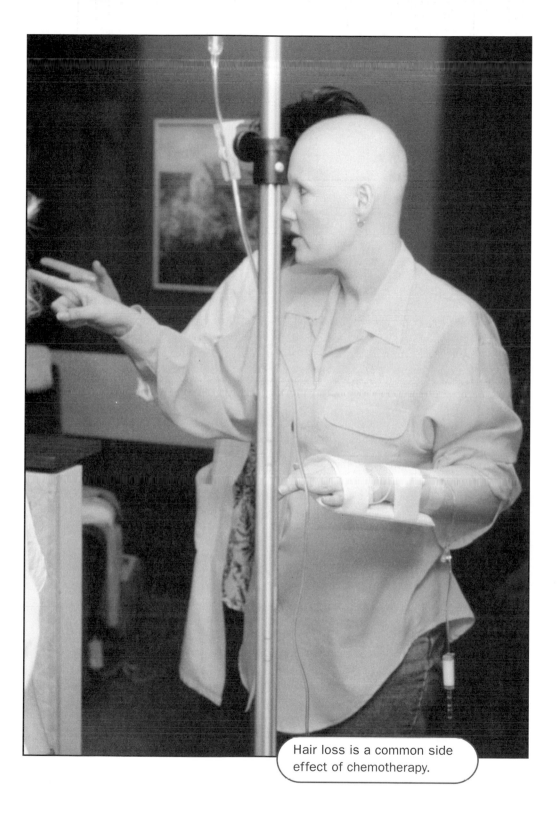

Hair loss is a common side effect of chemotherapy.

remission. The third, prophylactic therapy, is designed to prevent the recurrence of leukemia in the brain or spinal cord. Often chemotherapy is unable to completely kill the cancerous cells in those areas, so other forms of treatment, such as radiation, are necessary. The last stage is maintenance therapy. Its purpose is to make sure that the cancer doesn't return. This treatment can last up to several years.

When chemotherapy begins, the patient may need to stay in the hospital for a short time. The anticancer drugs used are very powerful and the doctors need to watch the effects and make adjustments if necessary. After a while, depending on the types of drugs used, the patients may be able to get chemotherapy at home, in the doctor's office, in a clinic, or through a hospital outpatient program.

How Chemotherapy Works

Chemotherapy uses anticancer drugs to block the ability of leukemic cells to grow and reproduce, which eventually kills them. The drugs are carried through the bloodstream, reaching all parts of the body. They seek and destroy any rapidly dividing cells they find. Since cancer cells divide more quickly than most healthy cells, chemotherapy is very effective.

The type of drugs, dosages, and the length of treatment depend upon the type of leukemia and how far the disease has progressed. In general, AML treatment uses higher doses of chemotherapy over a shorter period of time, while ALL uses lower doses over a longer period. The chronic leukemias receive the mildest forms of drugs.

The most common way to receive chemotherapy is through a needle inserted into a vein, usually on the hand or lower arm. It can also be given through a catheter (a thin tube that is placed into a large vein in the body), or injected into a muscle. Some types of milder chemotherapy can be taken orally in pill, capsule, or liquid form. Others can be applied directly onto the skin.

Side Effects

Receiving chemotherapy usually does not hurt the patient. However, many people experience unpleasant side effects. While chemotherapy is effective in attacking the rapidly growing cancer cells, it also poisons healthy cells that grow quickly. These include cells in the bone marrow, the lining of the mouth and intestines, and the hair follicles. Typical side effects are hair loss, nausea, vomiting, and mouth sores. Other possible side effects include infections, fatigue, anemia, and an increased chance of bleeding.

The kidneys, liver, heart, and other organs can also be damaged. As chemotherapy does its job and the leukemic cells break down, they release certain products and minerals into the bloodstream that are dangerous to many organs. This occurrence is called tumor lysis. Throughout treatment, doctors carefully monitor the organs and try to prevent any permanent damage.

Once treatment ends, the healthy cells repair themselves and the side effects disappear. The amount of time it takes to recover depends upon the types of anticancer drugs taken, the dosages, and the length of time the drugs were given. Although the side effects may be unpleasant for the patient, it is important to remember that they are usually not permanent and that chemotherapy is the most effective way of treating leukemia.

"The first few weeks of chemotherapy were definitely the hardest," Paul said. His dad had been diagnosed with acute myelogenous leukemia and began chemotherapy the very next day. His doctors gave him very strong anticancer drugs through an IV hooked up to his arm. "It was so hard to watch him feel so sick and not be able to do anything to help. He looked so green and was throwing up all the time. He lost a ton of weight because nothing tasted good and just the smell of food made him nauseated. But it was worth it, because after those three weeks, we found out that the cancer was in remission."

Radiation

Radiation treatment uses high-energy particles or waves, such as X rays, gamma rays, and alpha and beta particles, to destroy cancer cells. It works by causing such severe damage to dividing cells that they self-destruct. Unlike chemotherapy, which spreads the anticancer treatment to all parts of the body, radiation is aimed directly at the abnormal cells. However, radiation cannot tell the difference between the cancer cells and healthy cells. Therefore, some normal cells in the immediate area are usually affected. Most healthy cells recover fully after treatment has ended.

In leukemia patients, radiation is used only to treat tumors or leukemic cells in certain parts of the body, usually the lymph nodes, spleen, brain, or the spine. Often chemotherapy alone often does not destroy all the cancerous cells in those areas.

There are two ways to receive radiation treatment: external and internal. To receive external radiation, the patient lies on a table under the radiation machine. The machine is carefully positioned so that the high energy rays are aimed directly at the cancer cells. When it is turned on, high doses of radiation damage the cancer cells so they can no longer grow, reproduce, and spread. Internal radiation uses a radioactive wire or pellet that is implanted near the tumor. This form of radiation is sometimes used after a tumor has been surgically

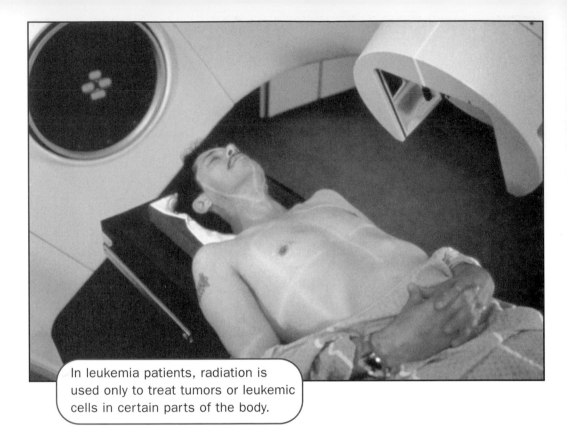

In leukemia patients, radiation is used only to treat tumors or leukemic cells in certain parts of the body.

removed to kill any cancerous cells that might remain.

As with chemotherapy, the doses of radiation and the number of treatments varies from person to person. The typical cycle is five days a week for five to eight weeks. The weekends are usually rest breaks that give the healthy cells a chance to recover.

Surgery

Although surgery is the oldest and most widely used treatment for cancer patients, it is usually not used for leukemia patients. For cancer to be surgically removed, it must be in the form of a solid tumor. Since leukemic cells can be found throughout the entire bloodstream, surgery is not an option. Sometimes a splenectomy may

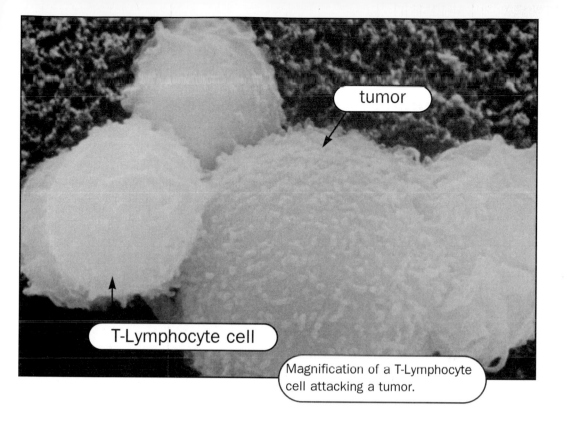

tumor

T-Lymphocyte cell

Magnification of a T-Lymphocyte cell attacking a tumor.

be performed to remove an enlarged spleen that is causing pain or discomfort to the patient.

Bone Marrow Transplant

If chemotherapy is not successful or if the leukemia returns after treatment, a bone marrow transplant may be considered. During a transplant, the patient's unhealthy bone marrow is replaced with normal marrow.

The patient's health must be carefully evaluated. Some patients may not be eligible for a transplant. For example, in people over the age of fifty-five, the risk of a transplant usually outweighs the possible benefit.

If the patient is a good candidate for a transplant, a suitable donor must be found. Often this is the hardest part of a bone marrow transplant. The donor must have the same proteins in the WBCs as the patient. An identical twin is the ideal donor because his or her genes are an exact duplicate of the patient's. Brothers or sisters are sometimes also good matches. If no family member is a match, people can search the National Marrow Donor Program. This is a listing of volunteers who would be willing to donate their marrow if they are a good match.

Sometimes doctors are able to collect the patient's own bone marrow while the leukemia is in remission. It is treated with chemotherapy drugs to remove any cancer cells that might remain and then stored in case the cancer returns and a bone marrow transplant is needed. This relatively new procedure is quite successful because it eliminates the possibility that the body will reject the healthy marrow as foreign material.

The first step in the transplant procedure is to destroy the patient's own leukemic marrow with high doses of drugs. Then his or her immune system is weakened so it won't reject the new cells. Although this is a necessary step, it leaves the person in a vulnerable state because he or she is unable to fight infections. The patient will probably be kept in isolation in a hospital during this time to decrease the risk.

The healthy bone marrow is removed from the donor's hipbone. It is then injected into the leukemia patient's bloodstream. It travels through the blood and enters the marrow through cavities in the bones. There is a chance that the patient's body will reject the transplanted marrow. Or, in some cases, the donated marrow makes the patient ill. Doctors keep the patient in the hospital and watch carefully for signs of rejection. If the transplant is successful, the number of platelets and granulocytes in the patient's blood will increase. The new marrow will begin to produce new blood cells about a month after the procedure.

Supportive Therapy

While patients receive treatment for leukemia, they also receive treatments that protect them from infections and illnesses. These treatments are called supportive therapy. Supportive therapy is necessary because the patients do not have as many healthy blood cells and are susceptible to infections, anemia, and bleeding.

It is normal for patients to receive blood transfusions during treatment. Some people need fresh blood two or three times a week. The transfusions help keep the blood count as normal as possible.

Precautions will be taken to protect the patient from infections. Visitors may be asked to wash their hands and put on a plastic apron before entering the room. People with a cough or a cold will not be allowed to see the patient. If the patient develops an infection, he or she is given antibiotics. The antibiotics help the body destroy foreign bacteria and boost the immune system.

If the immune system becomes extremely weak, the patient may be kept in an isolation ward.

A possible side effect from chemotherapy might be mouth or throat sores, which make it difficult to eat. If this occurs, the doctors usually begin feeding the patient intravenously (with an IV). It is important that the patient receive good nutrition to stay as healthy as possible.

Many patients have a Hickman line inserted into the chest. A Hickman line is a narrow plastic tube through which blood samples can be taken, drugs given, and blood transfusions made. It avoids the need to repeatedly puncture the veins and makes the process more comfortable for the patient.

Remission

The aim of all treatments for cancer is to bring about a complete remission. When cancer is in complete remission, it means that the patient has no symptoms and laboratory tests show no signs of the disease anywhere in the body. A partial remission is when the patient responds well to treatment, but there is still evidence of the disease.

In remission, there is still a chance that a leukemic cell has managed to survive undetected and will start to reproduce. Only time can tell if this is the case. If there is still no sign of leukemia after five years, the patient is considered cured.

The five-year survival rate for leukemia in adults is 42 percent. For children, the five-year survival rate is now 80 percent. These numbers have improved dramatically over the decades. In 1960, only 14 percent of patients survived for five years.

Chapter Four

After Treatment

During the first few years after treatment, it is very important for the patient to have regular checkups. Blood and bone marrow tests are performed to make sure that the blood count and cells are normal. The doctors also watch for short- and long-term side effects of the treatment. They want to be certain that no permanent damage has been done. The patient needs to inform the doctor if he or she is having any unusual symptoms, such as bleeding that won't stop, bone or joint pain, fatigue, or paleness.

Deb can always tell when it's time for her little sister Laura's checkup. Laura's case of ALL went into remission two years ago and her follow-up appointments now are scheduled every six months. During the months between visits, it is easy to forget that Laura ever had leukemia. But around the time of the appointment, everyone becomes really tense. They worry that the doctor will tell them that the cancer has come back.

The week before the appointment everyone watches Laura carefully. Deb knows her parents don't sleep because she can often hear them talking late into the night. Deb is always extra nice to Laura and lets her play with her things.

The family doesn't relax until after the results of the tests come back a few days after the exam. So far, Laura's blood count has been normal and there are no signs of the disease. But until five years have passed, they know that the leukemia could come back at any time.

Relapse

If the cancer cells return after a partial or complete remission, it is called a relapse. The relapse could occur while the patient is still receiving treatment, because the cancer cells become resistant to the treatment being used. Or it could occur years after treatment has ended, because not all the cancer cells were killed the first time. Relapses are harder to treat because the body may have become resistant to certain anticancer drugs. Switching to a different combination of drugs may put the cancer into remission again. However, the odds of beating the cancer after a relapse are less favorable.

Six months after Kevin's leukemia went into remission, doctors discovered that leukemic blasts had returned to his bone marrow during a follow-up visit. He started chemotherapy again with a different combination of drugs. It was hard for him to keep a positive attitude because he thought that he had already beat the disease. And he was upset that he had to deal with the side effects, like losing his hair and feeling nauseated again. But the inconvenience was worth it. He has been cancer-free for three years now and plans to graduate from high school next year.

Chapter Five

Emotional Aspects of Dealing with Leukemia

If someone close to you has been diagnosed with leukemia, you are dealing with some very difficult issues. You may not have ever known anyone who was facing a life-threatening illness before and may be confused about what to do. Remember that there is no "right" way to act or feel. Everyone deals with difficult times in his or her own way. Any emotion you have is completely valid, even if it is different from what other people feel.

Denial is a common occurrence when a disease is diagnosed. At first, it is difficult to imagine what is going to happen in the future. It is often easier for people to deny the problem while they adjust to the idea. Up to a certain point, this is a healthy reaction, but it can become dangerous if it affects the patient's treatment. It

49

is important to accept the diagnosis and begin dealing with the reality of leukemia.

Steve's mother is worried about her coworker, Linda, a single mom with a three-year-old daughter. A month ago Linda's daughter was diagnosed with acute lymphocytic leukemia (ALL). The doctor told her that her daughter was very ill and needed to begin chemotherapy immediately. Linda refused to believe that her daughter had leukemia and took her to other doctors for different opinions. Everyone gave the same diagnosis. Despite pleadings from the health professionals and her friends, Linda still refuses to believe the doctors and is avoiding admitting her daughter to the hospital. "That poor little girl," Steve's mother said. "By the time Linda realizes how sick her daughter is, it may be too late."

After denial, people often feel angry. They may feel angry at God for letting this disease happen to a loved one. Or they may be mad at the medical professionals for not knowing all the answers and not having a certain cure. Often this anger gets directed mistakenly at family members or friends. If you find yourself feeling angry, it is important to recognize the source of this emotion so that you do not take it out on others. At the same time, if someone else is upset, it may help to

After denial, people often feel angry.

remember that this is a normal response. He or she is probably feeling helpless and angry about the disease.

A diagnosis of any disease causes fear in most people. They are afraid of the future, afraid that they won't have the strength to handle the situation, and afraid about what others might think. The best way to deal with fear is to talk about it. Once other people are aware of your concerns, they will be able to help you deal with it.

You also may be feeling helpless if someone you know has been diagnosed with leukemia. It can be discouraging that so many things about the disease are not understood and that no one knows if a treatment is going to work. While it is difficult not to know what will happen in the future, there are a few things you can do right now to make yourself feel better about the situation. Here are four tips to help you cope when someone you know has been diagnosed.

First, educate yourself about the disease. You have already started by reading this book. But make sure that you don't stop there. Ask questions, talk to the doctors, and read other books. A good source of current information is the Internet. But remember that anyone can place information on the Web, even if it is wrong. Be sure to use sites from reputable hospitals and organizations. A list of organizations and Web sites is given at the end of this book. If you learn all you can about the disease, the diagnosis won't seem as overwhelming.

Educating yourself about the disease is one way to cope with Leukomia.

Secondly, have a strong support system. Families dealing with leukemia often feel very isolated. It usually helps to meet other people who are going through the same thing. Then you have others with whom to share your experiences. Support groups can be a big help. These are often set up in the hospital or by other organizations, such as the Leukemia Society of America (LSA) or the American Cancer Society (ACS). If you are feeling like no one understands what you are going through, reach out to people. No one should go through a difficult time alone.

The third tip is to take good care of yourself. Going through such a stressful time is hard on your body. Be sure to get enough sleep, proper nutrition,

Having a strong, positive philosophy of life can get you through tough times.

and exercise. Being in good shape mentally and physically will help you and others deal with the emotions and issues involved.

"When my cousin was diagnosed with leukemia, my aunt and uncle sort of fell apart," said eighteen-year-old Sarah. "Luckily it was summer vacation, so I could spend a lot of time at the hospital with them. I noticed that they weren't eating regularly, so I brought fresh fruit, bagels, and muffins in the morning, and sandwiches at lunch. At such a stressful time it is easy to forget to eat, but it is important to keep up your strength. I also felt better because I was doing something helpful for the family."

The final tip is to have a strong, positive philosophy of life. For some people this is found in religion. For others, it is simply a certain mindset or positive way of thinking. This powerful force often helps people to remain hopeful in the most difficult times and to keep a good perspective on life.

Despite all the tough times that follow a diagnosis of leukemia, many people feel that the experience can also have a positive effect. They become closer to supportive family members, friends, and medical professionals. They meet many brave people who share their knowledge and experience. They learn to appreciate what they have and to not take things for granted. But most of all, they develop a strong belief in the value of life.

Glossary

acute leukemia A type of leukemia that progresses quickly if left untreated.

acute lymphocytic leukemia (ALL) A type of leukemia that is fast developing and affects the lymphocytes. It is the most common form of childhood leukemia.

acute myelogenous leukemia (AML) A type of leukemia that is fast developing and affects the monocytes or granulocytes. It is the second most common form in children.

anemia A condition in which there are too few red blood cells in the bloodstream. Not enough oxygen gets carried throughout the body, causing the patient to become tired and pale.

bone marrow A soft, fatty substance that fills the insides of bones. Blood cells are created in the bone marrow.

bone marrow aspiration A method used to draw out bone marrow from the body.

bone marrow transplant When the patient's unhealthy bone marrow is replaced with healthy bone marrow from a donor.

chemotherapy A type of treatment for cancer in which anticancer drugs travel throughout the bloodstream and destroy all rapidly dividing cells.

chronic leukemia   A type of leukemia that is slow to progress. Chronic leukemia is more common in adults than children.

chronic lymphocytic leukemia (CLL)   A type of leukemia that is slow to progress and affects the lymphocytes.

chronic myeloid leukemia (CML)   A type of leukemia that is slow to progress and affects the monocytes or granulocytes.

granulocytes   A type of white blood cell that contains enzymes that break down foreign material.

hematologist   A doctor who specializes in blood diseases.

immune system   The body's natural defense system against germs, infections, and illnesses.

lymphoblasts or blasts   Abnormal, immature white blood cells.

lymphocytes   A type of white blood cell that makes substances to fight foreign material.

monocyte   A type of white blood cell that destroys foreign material.

oncogene   A type of gene that has the potential to turn normal cells into cancerous ones.

oncologist   A doctor who specializes in the treatment of cancer.

platelet   A type of blood cell that forms plugs to stop bleeding from injury.

red blood cell (RBC)   A type of blood cell that carries oxygen around the body and helps remove carbon dioxide.

relapse   When signs of a disease return after a remission.

remission   When there are no longer signs of the disease in the patient's body.

tumor lysis   When products and minerals are released into the bloodstream as cancer cells break down during chemotherapy. It can be dangerous to many organs.

white blood cell (WBC)   A type of blood cell that fights infections.

Where to Go for Help

There are many organizations in the United States and around the world that specialize in cancer care. Some focus on researching new drugs and treatments, some try to find the causes of cancer, and others create support groups for patients and families. Great strides have been made in the past few decades in developing effective treatments. With continuing research, we can hope to be able to cure all forms of leukemia in the future.

The American Cancer Society (ACS) is a nationwide organization dedicated to fighting cancer through research and education. They have 3,400 offices in all fifty states and Puerto Rico. The ACS is an excellent source of information on both childhood and adult leukemia. To find your local chapter, you can call 1-800-ACS-2345 or check their Web site at *http://www.cancer.org*.

The Candlelighters Childhood Cancer Foundation was founded in 1970 by parents of children with cancer. Its membership is over 43,000 and includes parents, patients, family members, and health care professionals. They offer support groups in all U.S. states and in many countries around the world and have published many books and pamphlets discussing leukemia in children. For more information call 1-800-366-2223 or check the Web site *http://www.candlelighters.org*.

The Leukemia Society of America (LSA) is a national health agency dedicated to finding the cause, treatments, and cures for leukemia, Hodgkin's disease, non-Hodgkin's lymphoma, and multiple myeloma. It was started in 1949 by parents whose son died of leukemia. They realized the need for an organization dedicated to leukemia and related diseases. It has fifty-seven chapters throughout the country. Their Web site is *http://www.leukemia.org* and the phone number is 1-800-955-4LSA.

The National Cancer Institute (NCI) is a federal organization that coordinates the government's cancer research. It is part of the research institutes and centers at the National Institute of Health in Washington DC. They can provide information about research and new treatments. NCI can be reached at 1-800-4-CANCER or at the Web site *http://www.nci.nih.gov*.

For Further Reading

Bracken, Jeanne Munn. Children with Cancer: A
Comprehensive Reference Guide for Parents. New
York: Oxford University Press, 1986.

Buckman, Robert. *What You Really Need to Know
About Cancer: A Comprehensive Guide for Patients
and Their Families.* Baltimore: The Johns Hopkins
University Press, 1997.

Dollinger, Malin, M.D., Ernest H. Rosenbaum, M.D.,
and Greg Cable. *Everyone's Guide to Cancer
Therapy,* revised third ed. Kansas City: Andrews
McMeel Publishing, 1997.

Fine, Judylaine. *Afraid to Ask: A Book for Families to
Share About Cancer.* New York: Lothrop, Lee &
Shepard Books, 1984.

Jacoby, David B. *Encyclopedia of Family Health.* New
York: Marshall Cavendish, 1998.

Monroe, Judy. *The Facts About Leukemia.* New York: Crestwood House, 1990.

Rodgers, Joann Ellison. *Cancer.* New York: Chelsea House Publishers, 1990.

The American Medical Association Family Medical Guide, Third Edition. New York: Random House, 1994.

The World Book Encyclopedia. Chicago: World Book, Inc., 1999.

Web Sites

The Child Leukemia Resource Center
American Cancer Society
http://www.cancer.org

Leukemia Society of America
http://www.leukemia.org

Index

About the Author
Heather Moehn is a freelance writer of books for young adults. She lives in Boston, Massachusetts.

Photo Credits

Cover © International Stock. P. 2 © AP/Worldwide; pp. 8, 13, 19, 30, 35, 40, 41 © Custom Medical Stock Photo; p. 15 by John Bentham; p. 33, 51, 53 by Brian Silak; p. 25 © Skjold; p. 26 © Corbis; p. 54 by Seth Dinnerman.